Born in 1941

by

Kerry Butters.

Born in 1941.

Millennium:	2nd millennium
Centuries:	19th century – **20th century** – 21st century
Decades:	1910s 1920s 1930s – **1940s** – 1950s 1960s 1970s
Years:	1938 1939 1940 – **1941** – 1942 1943 1944

1941 (MCMXLI) was a common year starting on Wednesday (dominical letter E) of the Gregorian calendar, the 1941st year of the Common Era (CE) and *Anno Domini* (AD) designations, the 941st year of the 2nd millennium, the 41st year of the 20th century, and the 2nd year of the 1940s decade.

Contents

Events

January

- January–August – 10,072 men, women and children with mental and physical disabilities are asphyxiated with carbon monoxide in a gas chamber at Hadamar Euthanasia Centre in Nazi Germany in the first phase of mass killings under the Action T4 program here.
- January 1 – Thailand Prime Minister Plaek Phibunsongkhram decrees January 1 as the official start of the Thai solar calendar new year (thus the previous year that began April 1 had only 9 months).
- January 3 – A decree (*Normalschrifterlass*) promulgated in Nazi Germany by Martin Bormann on behalf of Adolf Hitler requires replacement of blackletter typefaces by Antiqua.
- January 4 – The short subject *Elmer's Pet Rabbit* is released, marking the second appearance of Bugs Bunny, and also the first to have his name on a title card.

- January 5 – WWII: At the Battle of Bardia in Libya, Australian and British troops defeat Italian forces, the first battle of the war in which an Australian Army formation takes part.
- January 6 – The keel of the USS *Missouri* is laid at the New York Navy Yard in Brooklyn.
- January 10 – The Lend-Lease Act is introduced into the United States Congress.
- January 11 – The British Royal Navy light cruiser HMS *Southampton* (83) is sunk off Malta.
- January 13 – All persons born in Puerto Rico since this day are declared U.S. citizens by birth, through U.S. federal law.
- January 14 – WWII: Commerce raiding German auxiliary cruiser *Pinguin* captures the Norwegian whaling fleet near Bouvet Island, effectively ending Southern Ocean whaling for the duration of the war.
- January 15 – John Vincent Atanasoff and Clifford Berry describe the workings of the Atanasoff–Berry computer in print.
- January 19 – WWII: British troops attack Italian-held Eritrea.
- January 20 – Chief Justice Charles Evans Hughes swears in U.S. President Franklin D. Roosevelt for his third term.
- January 22
  - WWII: Battle of Tobruk: Australian and British forces capture Tobruk from the Italians.
  - In Sweden, Victor Hasselblad registers the Hasselblad camera company.
- January 23 – Aviator Charles Lindbergh testifies before the U.S. Congress and recommends that the United States negotiate a neutrality pact with Adolf Hitler.

- January 27 – WWII: Joseph Grew, the U.S. ambassador to Japan, reports to Washington a rumor overheard at a diplomatic reception concerning a planned surprise attack on Pearl Harbor, Hawaii.
- January 30 – WWII: Australians capture Derna, Libya, from the Italians.

February

- February 3 – WWII: The Nazis forcibly restore Pierre Laval to office in occupied Vichy France.
- February 4 – WWII: The United Service Organization (USO) is created to entertain American troops.
- February 5 – Air Training Corps: The Air Training Corps is formed in the United Kingdom.
- February 5–April 1 – WWII: Battle of Keren – British and Free French Forces fight hard to capture the strategic town of Keren in Italian Eritrea.
- February 6 – WWII: Fall of Benghazi to the Western Desert Force. Lieutenant-General Erwin Rommel is appointed commander of Afrika Korps.
- February 8 – WWII: The U.S. House of Representatives passes the Lend-Lease Act.
- February 9 – Winston Churchill, in a worldwide broadcast, tells the United States to show its support by sending arms to the British: "Give us the tools, and we will finish the job."
- February 12
  - WWII: Erwin Rommel arrives in Tripoli.
  - Reserve Constable Albert Alexander, a patient at the Radcliffe Infirmary in Oxford, becomes the first person

treated with penicillin intravenously, by Howard
Florey's team. He reacts positively but there is
insufficient supply of the drug to reverse his terminal
infection. A successful treatment is achieved during
May.

- February 13 – Aircraft from HMS *Formidable* attack Massawa
in Eritrea.
- February 14 – WWII: Admiral Kichisaburō Nomura begins
his duties as Japanese Ambassador to the United States.
- February 19–22 – WWII: Three Nights' Blitz over Swansea,
South Wales: Over these 3 nights of intensive bombing,
which lasted a total of 13 hours and 48 minutes, Swansea's
town centre is almost completely obliterated by the 896 high
explosive bombs employed by the Luftwaffe; 397 casualties
and 230 deaths reported.
- February 22 – WWII: HMS *Shropshire* bombards Barawa, on
the coast between Kismayo and Mogadishu.
- February 23 – Glenn T. Seaborg isolates and discovers
plutonium.
- February 25 – WWII:
  - The occupied Netherlands starts the first popular
  uprising in Europe against the Axis powers, the
  "February strike" against German deportation of Jews
  in Amsterdam and surroundings.
  - British submarine HMS *Upright* attacks an Italian
  convoy sinking the cruiser *Armando Diaz*.
- February 27 – WWII: The New Zealand Division cruiser
HMS *Leander* (1931) sinks Italian armed merchant raider
Ramb I off the Maldives.

March

- March 1
  - WWII: Bulgaria signs the Tripartite Pact, thus joining the Axis powers.
  - W47NV begins operations in Nashville, Tennessee, becoming the first FM radio station.
  - Arthur L. Bristol becomes Rear Admiral for the United States Navy's Support Force, Atlantic Fleet.
- March 4 – WWII: Operation Claymore – British Commandos carry out a successful raid on the Lofoten Islands off the north coast of Norway.
- March 8 – WWII: The U.S. Senate passes the Lend-Lease Act.
- March 11 – WWII: Franklin D. Roosevelt, President of the United States, signs the Lend-Lease Act into law, providing for the U.S. to provide Lend-Lease aid to the Allies.
- March 15 – Richard C. Hottelet is arrested by the Gestapo on "suspicion of espionage", but eventually released in July as part of a prisoner exchange with the U.S.
- March 16 – A group of U.S. warships arrive in Auckland, New Zealand, on a goodwill visit. On March 20, they arrive in Sydney, Australia.
- March 17
  - In Washington, D.C., the National Gallery of Art is officially opened by President Franklin D. Roosevelt.
  - British Minister of Labour Ernest Bevin calls for women to fill vital jobs.
- March 22 – Washington state's Grand Coulee Dam begins to generate electricity.

- March 24 – WWII: Rommel launches his first offensive in Cyrenaica.
- March 25 – WWII: The Kingdom of Yugoslavia joins the Axis powers in Vienna.
- March 27 – WWII:
  - Battle of Cape Matapan: Off the Peloponnese coast in the Mediterranean, British naval forces defeat those of Italy, sinking 5 warships. Battle ends on March 29.
  - An anti-Axis coup d'état in Yugoslavia forces Prince Paul into exile; 17-year-old King Peter II assumes power.
  - Japanese spy Takeo Yoshikawa arrives in Honolulu to study the Pacific Fleet at Pearl Harbor in preparation for a future attack.
- March 30 – WWII:
  - All German, Italian and Danish ships anchored in United States waters are taken into "protective custody".
  - A German Lorenz cipher machine operator sends a 4,000-character message twice, allowing British mathematician Bill Tutte to decipher the machine's coding mechanism.

April

- April – The Valley of Geysers is discovered on the Kamchatka Peninsula of Russia by Tatyana Ustinova.
- April 4 – WWII: Axis forces capture Benghazi.
- April 6 – WWII: Germany invades Yugoslavia and Greece.

- April 9 – The U.S. acquires full military defense rights in Greenland.
- April 10 – WWII:
  - The U.S. destroyer USS *Niblack*, while picking up survivors from a sunken Dutch freighter, drops depth charges on a German U-boat (the first "shot in anger" fired by America against Germany).
  - The Independent State of Croatia, a puppet state of the Axis powers, is established with Ustaše leader Ante Pavelić as head (*Poglavnik*) of the government.
- April 12 – WWII: German troops enter Belgrade.
- April 13 – Soviet–Japanese Neutrality Pact signed.
- April 15 – WWII: Axis forces reach Halfaya Pass on the Libyan-Egyptian frontier.
- April 17 – WWII: The Yugoslav Royal Army capitulates.
- April 18 – WWII: Prime Minister of Greece Alexandros Koryzis commits suicide as German troops approach Athens.
- April 19 – Bertolt Brecht's anti-war play *Mother Courage and Her Children* (German: *Mutter Courage und ihre Kinder*) receives its first theatrical production at the Schauspielhaus Zürich.
- April 21 – WWII: Greece capitulates. Commonwealth troops and some elements of the Greek Army withdraw to Crete.
- April 23 – The America First Committee holds its first mass rally in New York City, with Charles Lindbergh as keynote speaker.
- April 25 – Franklin D. Roosevelt, at his regular press conference, criticizes Charles Lindbergh by comparing him to the Copperheads of the Civil War period. In response,

Lindbergh resigns his commission in the U.S. Army Air Corps Reserve on April 28.

- April 27 – WWII: German troops enter Athens.

May

- May 1
  - The breakfast cereal *Cheerios* is introduced as *CheeriOats* by General Mills.
  - Orson Welles' film *Citizen Kane* premieres in New York City.
  - The first Defense Bonds and Defense Savings Stamps go on sale in the United States, to help fund the greatly increased production of military equipment.
- May 2 – Anglo-Iraqi War: British combat operations against the rebel government of Rashid Ali in the Kingdom of Iraq begin.
- May 5 – WWII: Emperor Haile Selassie enters Addis Ababa, which has been liberated from Italian forces; this date is subsequently commemorated as Liberation Day in Ethiopia.
- May 6 – At California's March Field, entertainer Bob Hope performs his first USO Show.
- May 8 – WWII: The German auxiliary cruiser *Pinguin* is sunk by HMS *Cornwall* (56) in the Indian Ocean.
- May 9 – WWII: The German submarine *U-110* is captured by the British Royal Navy. On board is the latest Enigma cryptography machine, which Allied cryptographers later use to break coded German messages.
- May 10

- WWII: The British House of Commons is damaged by the Luftwaffe in an air raid.
- Rudolf Hess parachutes into Scotland, claiming to be on a peace mission.
- May 11/May 12 – WWII: The Ustaše massacre 260–373 Serb men in a Catholic church in Glina, Croatia where the men had assembled to be received into the Catholic faith in exchange for their lives.
- May 12 – Konrad Zuse presents the Z3, the world's first working programmable, fully automatic computer, in Berlin.
- May 15
  - The first British jet aircraft, the Gloster E.28/39, is flown.
  - Joe DiMaggio's 56-game hitting streak begins as the New York Yankees' center fielder goes one for four against Chicago White Sox Pitcher Eddie Smith.
- May 19 – The Viet Minh is formed in at Pác Bó in Vietnam to overthrow French rule of the nation as an alliance between the Indochina Communist party, led by Ho Chi Minh, and the Nationalist party. It will become the Viet Cong during the Vietnam War.
- May 20 – WWII: The Battle of Crete begins as Germany launches an airborne invasion of Crete.
- May 21 – German submarine *U-69* (1940) sinks the U.S.-flagged SS *Robin Moor* off the west African coast, having allowed the passengers and crew to disembark.
- May 24
  - WWII: In the North Atlantic, German battleship *Bismarck* sinks battlecruiser HMS *Hood*, killing all but 3 crewmen from a total of 1,418 aboard the pride of the Royal Navy.

- The British submarine HMS *Upholder* torpedoes and sinks the Italian ocean liner SS *Conte Rosso*.
- May 26 – WWII: In the North Atlantic, Fairey Swordfish aircraft from the carrier HMS *Ark Royal* cripple the steering of German battleship *Bismarck* in an aerial torpedo attack.
- May 27
  - WWII: Franklin D. Roosevelt, President of the United States, proclaims an "unlimited national emergency."
  - WWII: German battleship *Bismarck* is sunk in the North Atlantic, killing 2,300. It is eventually found in 1989.
  - The Swiss Socialist Federation is banned.
- May 30 – WWII: Manolis Glezos and Apostolos Santas tear down the Nazi swastika on the Acropolis in Athens, and replace it with the Greek flag.
- May 31 – Anglo-Iraqi War: British troops complete the re-occupation of the Kingdom of Iraq, returning Prince 'Abd al-Ilah to power as regent for Faisal II.

June

- June 5
  - Four thousand Chongqing residents are asphyxiated in a bomb shelter during the Bombing of Chongqing.
  - A Serbian ammunition depot explodes at Smederevo on the outskirts of Belgrade, Serbia, killing 2,500, and injuring over 4,500.
- June 8 – WWII: British and Free French forces invade Syria.
- June 13 – TASS, the official Soviet news agency, denies reports of tension between Germany and the Soviet Union.
- June 14

- Soviet officials deport about 65,000 people from Estonia, Latvia and Lithuania to Siberia.
- All German and Italian assets in the United States are frozen.
- June 16
  - All German and Italian consulates in the United States are ordered closed and their staffs to leave the country by July 10.
  - WWII: British Fleet Air Arm aircraft sink the Vichy French ship *Chevalier Paul*.
- June 20
  - United States Army Air Corps becomes the United States Army Air Forces.
  - Walt Disney's live-action animated feature, *The Reluctant Dragon*, is released.
- June 22
  - WWII and Operation Barbarossa: Germany invades the Soviet Union.
  - WWII: Winston Churchill promises all possible British assistance to the Soviet Union in a worldwide broadcast: "Any man or state who fights against Nazidom will have our aid. Any man or state who marches with Hitler is our foe."
  - WWII: Italy and Romania declare war on the Soviet Union.
  - WWII: The First Sisak Partisan Brigade, the first anti-fascist armed unit in occupied Europe, is founded by Yugoslav partisans near Sisak, Croatia.
  - WWII: June Uprising in Lithuania and establishment of a Provisional Government of Lithuania begun by the

Lithuanian Activist Front in an attempt to liberate
Lithuania from Soviet occupation.

- June 23 – WWII: Hungary and Slovakia declare war on the
Soviet Union.
- June 24 – The Soviet Information Bureau, predecessor of RIA
Novosti, is founded.
- June 25 – WWII: Finland as a co-belligerent with Germany
attacks the Soviet Union to start the Continuation War.
- June 28 – WWII: Albania declares war on the Soviet Union.
- June 29 – WWII: Hitler's second-in-command Reichsmarshall
Hermann Göring is appointed as Hitler's successor in a
written decree. The decree will come into effect should
Hitler die in the middle of the war. (The decree becomes
void in April 1945 after Göring tries to assume power while
Hitler is still alive, leading to Göring's expulsion from the
Nazi Party.)

July

- July – The British Army's Special Air Service is formed.
- July 1
  - Commercial TV authorized by the FCC.
  - NBC television begins commercial operation on WNBT
    on channel 1. The world's first legal TV commercial, for
    Bulova watches, occurs at 2:29 PM over WNBT before a
    baseball game between the Brooklyn Dodgers and
    Philadelphia Phillies. The 10-second spot displays a
    picture of a clock superimposed on a map of the United
    States, accompanied by the voice-over "America runs
    on Bulova time." As a one-off special, the first quiz

show called "Uncle Bee" is telecast on WNBT's inaugural broadcast day, followed later the same day by Ralph Edwards hosting the second game show broadcast on U.S. television, *Truth or Consequences*, as simulcast on radio and TV and sponsored by Ivory soap. Weekly broadcasts of the show commence in 1956, with Bob Barker.

  - CBS television begins commercial operation on New York station WCBW (modern-day WCBS-TV) on channel 2.
- July 2 – WWII: Empire of Japan calls up 1 million men for military service.
- July 3 – WWII: Joseph Stalin, in his first address since the German invasion, calls upon the Soviet people to carry out a "scorched earth" policy of resistance to the bitter end.
- July 4 – The Holocaust: The massacre of Polish scientists and writers is committed by Nazi German troops in the occupied Polish city of Lwów.
- July 5 – WWII:
  - Operation Barbarossa: German troops reach the Dnieper River.
  - British troopship SS *Anselm* is torpedoed and sunk by German submarine *U-96* in the Atlantic Ocean with the loss of around 250 out of about 1310 on board.
- July 5–31: War is fought between Peru and Ecuador.
- July 7 – WWII: American forces take over the defense of Iceland from the British.
- July 10 – The Holocaust: Jedwabne pogrom: Local ethnic Poles massacre at least 340 Jewish residents of Jedwabne in occupied Poland.

- July 11 – The Northern Rhodesian Labour Party holds its first congress in Nkana.
- July 13 – WWII: Montenegro starts the second popular uprising in Europe against the Axis powers (the first being the "February strike" of February 25 *(above)* in the Netherlands).
- July 14 – WWII: Vichy France signs armistice terms ending all fighting in Syria and Lebanon.
- July 17 – Joe DiMaggio's 56 game hitting streak ends.
- July 19
  - WWII: A BBC broadcast by "Colonel Britton" calls on the people of occupied Europe to resist the Nazis under the slogan "V for Victory".
  - The first episode *The Midnight Snack* in which Tom and Jerry are officially named, more than a year after their first production *Puss Gets the Boot*
- July 23 – WWII: Italian aircraft damage the British destroyer HMS *Fearless* which has to be sunk.
- July 25 – Introduction of postal codes in Germany.
- July 26 – WWII:
  - In response to the Japanese occupation of French Indochina, U.S. President Franklin D. Roosevelt orders the seizure of all Japanese assets in the United States.
  - General Douglas MacArthur is named commander of all U.S. forces in the Philippines; the Philippines Army is ordered nationalized by President Roosevelt.
- July 29 – The Vichy Regime signs the Protocol Concerning Joint Defense and Joint Military Cooperation with the Empire of Japan, giving the Japanese a total of eight airfields, allowing them greater troop presence and the use of the

Indochinese financial system in return for continued French autonomy.

- July 30 – WWII: The Holocaust: Glina massacre of July–August 1941 – The Ustaše brutally kill 200 Serbs inside a Serbian Orthodox church in Glina, Croatia, with a total of 700–1,200 being killed in the area of the next few days.
- July 31 – WWII: The Holocaust: Under instructions from Adolf Hitler, Nazi official Hermann Göring orders S.S. General Reinhard Heydrich to "submit to me as soon as possible a general plan of the administrative material and financial measures necessary for carrying out the desired Final Solution of the Jewish question."

August

- August – Political Warfare Executive is formed in the United Kingdom.
- August 1 – First production Willys MB U.S. Army Jeep.
- August 5 – Provisional Government of Lithuania dissolved.
- August 6 – Six-year-old Elaine Esposito goes to have an appendix operation in Florida and lapses into a coma, dying 37 years later, still comatose.
- August 7 – WWII: British submarine HMS *Severn* sinks an Italian Marconi-class submarine.
- August 9 – Franklin D. Roosevelt and Winston Churchill meet onboard ship at Naval Station Argentia, Newfoundland. The Atlantic Charter (released August 14), setting goals for postwar international cooperation, is created as a result.

- August 16 – HMS *Mercury* Royal Navy Signals School and Combined Signals School opens at Leydene, near Petersfield, Hampshire, England.
- August 22 – WWII: France: The German Occupation Authority announces that anyone working for or aiding the Free French will be sentenced to death.
- August 24
  - WWII: A Luftwaffe bomb hits the Estonian steamer *Eestirand* with 3,500 Soviet-mobilized Estonian men on board, killing 598 of them.
  - Adolf Hitler orders a halt to the Action T4 program, Nazi Germany's systematic euthanasia of the mentally ill and handicapped, due to protests from the churches. However, graduates of the program are then transferred to Nazi concentration camps where they continue the killings.
- August 25 – WWII: The Anglo-Soviet invasion of Iran begins.
- August 27 – WWII: Pierre Laval is shot in an assassination attempt at Versailles, France.
- August 28 – WWII:
  - German troops capture Tallinn, Estonia from the Soviet Union, while attacks on the evacuating Soviet ships leave more than 12,000 dead in one of the bloodiest naval battles of World War II. German forces will capture the entire Estonian territory by 6 December.
  - The Soviet Union announces blowing up of the massive Dnieper Hydroelectric Station and dam at Zaporizhia to prevent its capture by the Germans.

- August 30 – German Troopship Bahia Laura is sunk by the HMS Trident (N52), 450 are killed.
- August 31 – *The Great Gildersleeve* debuts on NBC Radio in the United States.

September

- September 3 – The Holocaust: *SS-Hauptsturmführer* Karl Fritzsch first uses the pesticide Zyklon B to execute Soviet prisoners of war *en masse* at Auschwitz concentration camp; eventually it will be used to kill about 1.2 million people.
- September 6 – The Holocaust: The requirement to wear the Star of David with the word "Jew" inscribed, is extended to all Jews over the age of 6 in German-occupied areas.
- September 8 – WWII: The Siege of Leningrad begins: German forces begin a siege against the Soviet Union's second-largest city, Leningrad. Stalin orders the Volga Germans deported to Siberia.
- September 11 – WWII: Charles Lindbergh, at an America First Committee rally in Des Moines, Iowa, accuses "the British, the Jewish, and the Roosevelt administration" of leading the United States toward war. Widespread condemnation of Lindbergh follows.
- September 12 – WWII: The first snowfall is reported on the Russian front.
    - Construction on the Pentagon Building begins.
    - Franklin Roosevelt gives a fireside chat on the USS Greer incident
- September 14 – The State of Vermont "declares war" on Germany, by defining the United States to be in "armed

conflict" in order to extend a wartime bonus to Vermonters in the service.

- September 15 – The Estonian Self-Administration, headed by Hjalmar Mäe, is appointed by the German military administration.
- September 16 – Rezā Shāh of Iran is forced to resign in favor of his son Mohammad Reza Pahlavi, under pressure from the United Kingdom and the Soviet Union.
- September 22 – The town of Reshetylivka in the Soviet Union is occupied by German forces.
- September 27 – The first liberty ship, the SS *Patrick Henry*, is launched at Baltimore.
- September 28 – WWII: The Drama Uprising against the Bulgarian occupation in northern Greece begins.
- September 29 – WWII: The Moscow Conference begins; U.S. representative Averell Harriman and British representative Lord Beaverbrook meet with Soviet foreign minister Molotov to arrange urgent assistance for Russia.
- September 29–September 30 – The Holocaust: Babi Yar massacre – German troops, assisted by Ukrainian police and local collaborators, kill 33,771 Jews.

October

- October 1
  - The Holocaust: The Nazi German Majdanek concentration camp (*Konzentrationslager Lublin*) opens in occupied Poland on the outskirts of the town Lublin. Between October 1941 and July 1944 at least 200,000 people will be killed in the camp.

- o New Zealand Division of the Royal Navy becomes the Royal New Zealand Navy
- October 2 – WWII: Operation Typhoon begins as Germany launches an all-out offensive against Moscow.
- October 7 – John Curtin becomes the 14th Prime Minister of Australia.
- October 8 – WWII: In their invasion of the Soviet Union, Germany reaches the Sea of Azov with the capture of Mariupol.
- October 11 – October 12 – Fire destroys a Firestone Tire & Rubber Co. plant in Fall River, Massachusetts, consuming 15,850 tons of rubber and causing a setback to the United States war effort.
- October 13 – The Holocaust: Heinrich Himmler instructs SS and Police Leader Odilo Globocnik to begin construction of Bełżec; the first of the Operation Reinhard extermination camps.
- October 15 – British submarine HMS *Torbay* bombards the port of Apollonia, Cyrenaica in Italian Libya.
- Mid-October – First production P-38E Lightning fighter produced by Lockheed.
- October 16 – WWII: The Soviet government moves to Kuibyshev (modern Samara), but Stalin remains in Moscow.
- October 17 – WWII: The destroyer USS *Kearny* is torpedoed and damaged near Iceland, killing 11 sailors (the first American military casualties of the war).
- October 18 – General Hideki Tōjō becomes the 40th Prime Minister of Japan.

- October 20–21 – WWII: Kragujevac massacre – German soldiers and local auxiliaries massacre more than 2000 civilian men at Kragujevac in Nazi-occupied Serbia.
- October 23 – Walt Disney's fourth animated film *Dumbo* is released.
- October 25 – Franz von Werra disappears during a flight over the North Sea.
- October 30 – WWII: Franklin D. Roosevelt, President of the United States, approves US$1 billion in Lend-Lease aid to the Soviet Union.
- October 31
  - WWII: The destroyer USS *Reuben James* is torpedoed by a German U-boat near Iceland, killing more than 100 United States Navy sailors.
  - Last day of carving on Mount Rushmore in South Dakota.

November

- November 5 – WWII: US Holds peace talks with Japan
- November 6 – WWII: Soviet leader Joseph Stalin addresses the Soviet Union for only the second time during his three-decade rule (the first time was earlier this year on July 2). He states that 350,000 Soviet troops have been killed in German attacks but that the Germans have lost 4.5 million soldiers (a gross exaggeration) and that Soviet victory is near.
- November 7 – WWII: The Soviet hospital ship *Armenia* is sunk by German aircraft while evacuating refugees, wounded military and the staff of several Crimean hospitals. It is estimated that more than 5,000 died in the sinking.

- November 10 – In a speech at the Mansion House, London, Winston Churchill promises "should the United States become involved in war with Japan, the British declaration will follow within the hour".
- November 12 – WWII:
  - As the Battle of Moscow begins, temperatures around Moscow drop to -12 °C, and the Soviet Union launches ski troops for the first time against the freezing German forces near the city.
  - The Soviet cruiser *Chervona Ukraina* is hit three times in the Severnaya Bay by bombs from German Junkers Ju 87 Stuka dive bombers from II./StG 77 during the Siege of Sevastopol.
- November 14 – WWII:
  - The British aircraft carrier HMS *Ark Royal* sinks under tow off Gibraltar after being torpedoed the previous day by German submarine *U-81*.
  - The Holocaust: In Slonim (Byelorussian SSR), German forces engaged in Operation Barbarossa murder 9000 Jews this day.
- November 17 – WWII: Joseph Grew, the United States ambassador to Japan, cables to Washington, D.C., a warning that Japan may strike suddenly and unexpectedly.
- November 18 – WWII: Operation Crusader, a British Eighth Army operation to relieve the Siege of Tobruk in North Africa, begins.
- November 19 – WWII: Both commerce raiding German auxiliary cruiser *Kormoran* and Australian cruiser HMAS *Sydney* sink following a battle off the coast of

Western Australia. There are no survivors from the 645 Australian sailors aboard *Sydney*.

- November 21 – The radio program *King Biscuit Time* is broadcast for the first time (it later becomes the longest running daily radio broadcast in history and the most famous live blues radio program).
- November 22 – WWII: HMS *Devonshire* sinks commerce raiding German auxiliary cruiser *Atlantis*, ending the longest warship cruise of the war (622 days without in-port replenishment or repair).
- November 26 – WWII:
  - The Hull note (Outline of Proposed Basis for Agreement Between the United States and Japan), named for Secretary of State Cordell Hull, is delivered to the Empire of Japan by the United States.
  - A fleet of 6 aircraft carriers commanded by Japanese Vice Admiral Chūichi Nagumo leaves Hitokapu Bay for Pearl Harbor under strict radio silence.
- November 27
  - WWII: Germans reach their closest approach to Moscow. They are subsequently frozen by cold weather and attacks by the Soviets.
  - A group of young men stop traffic on U.S. Highway 99 south of Yreka, California, handing out fliers proclaiming the establishment of the State of Jefferson.

December

- December 1 – WWII:
  - Fiorello La Guardia, Mayor of New York City and Director of the Office of Civilian Defense, signs Administrative Order 9, creating the Civil Air Patrol under the authority of the United States Army Air Forces.
  - A state of emergency is declared in British Malaya and the Straits Settlements.
- December 2 – WWII: The code message "Climb Mount Niitaka" is transmitted to the Japanese task force, indicating that negotiations have broken down and that the attack on Pearl Harbor is to be carried out according to plan.
- December 4 – The State of Jefferson is declared in Yreka, California, with a judge, John Childs, as governor.
- December 6 – WWII:
  - Soviet counterattacks begin against German troops encircling Moscow. The Wehrmacht is subsequently pushed back over 200 miles.
  - The United Kingdom declares war on Finland and Romania.
- December 6 – WWII: British submarine HMS *Perseus* is sunk by a mine off Cephalonia.
- December 7 (December 8 – 3:18 a.m., Japan Standard Time) – WWII:
  - Attack on Pearl Harbor: Aircraft flying from Imperial Japanese Navy carriers launch a surprise attack on the United States fleet at Pearl Harbor in Hawaii, thus drawing the United States into World War II. The

attack begins at 7:48 a.m. Hawaiian Standard Time and is announced on radio stations in the U.S. at about 11:26 p.m. PST (19.26 GMT).

- The Japanese declaration of war on the United States and the British Empire is published in Japanese evening newspapers but not formally delivered to the U.S. until the following day. Canada declares war on Japan.
- Tobruk's British and Commonwealth garrison is relieved after Axis forces under Rommel withdraw.

- December 8
  - WWII: The Battle of Hong Kong begins shortly after 8:00 a.m. (local time), less than eight hours after the attack on Pearl Harbor, when Japanese forces invade Hong Kong, which is defended by British, Canadian and local troops. The United Kingdom officially declares war on the Empire of Japan.
  - WWII: Japanese Invasion of Shanghai International Settlement, Began to occupy the British and the American sectors after the attack on Pearl Harbor.
  - WWII: The Japanese occupation of the Philippines begins ten hours after the attack on Pearl Harbor when Japanese forces invade Luzon and destroy U.S. aircraft on Clark Field.
  - WWII: President of the United States Franklin D. Roosevelt delivers his "Infamy Speech" to a Joint session of the United States Congress at 12:30 p.m. EST (17.30 GMT). Transmitted live over all four major national networks it attracts the largest audience ever for an American radio broadcast, over 81% of homes. Within an hour, Congress agrees to the

President's request for a United States declaration of war upon Japan and he signs it at 4:10 p.m.

- ○ WWII: Australia, New Zealand, The Netherlands, the Free French, Yugoslavia, Costa Rica, Cuba, El Salvador, Guatemala and Honduras also officially declare war on Japan, and the Republic of China declares war on the Axis powers.
- ○ WWII: Japanese also attack British Malaya and Thailand.
- ○ WWII: The German advance on Moscow (Operation Typhoon) is suspended for the winter.
- ○ The Holocaust: the Nazi German Chełmno extermination camp opens in occupied Poland near the village of Chełmno nad Nerem. Between December 1941-April 1943 and June 1944-January 1945 at least 153,000 people will be killed in the camp.
- ○ The Holocaust The first mass gassing of Jews began in Chełmno extermination camp on 8 December 1941, when the Nazis used gas vans to murder people from the Lodz ghetto.

- December 10 – WWII:
  - ○ The British battleship HMS *Prince of Wales* and battlecruiser HMS *Repulse* are sunk by Japanese aircraft in the South China Sea north of Singapore.
  - ○ The Provisional Government of the Republic of Korea officially declares war on Japan.
- December 11 – WWII:
  - ○ Germany and Italy declare war on the United States. The U.S. responds in kind.

- Mildred Gillars ("Axis Sally") delivers her first propaganda broadcast to Allied troops.
- December 12 – WWII:
  - Hungary and Romania declare war on the United States.
  - British India declares war on the Empire of Japan.
  - The United States seizes the French ship SS *Normandie*.
  - The Kimura Detachment of the Japanese Imperial forces is occupied in Legaspi, Albay, Philippines.
- December 13 – Sweden's low temperature record of -53 °C is set in a village within the Vilhelmina Municipality.
- December 14 – WWII: The Independent State of Croatia declares war on the United States and the United Kingdom.
- December 19 – WWII:
  - Hitler becomes Supreme Commander-in-Chief of the German Army.
  - Twelve days after the Japanese raid on Pearl Harbor, the United States Naval Academy in Annapolis, Maryland graduates its "Class of 1942" a semester early so as to induct the graduating students without delay into the U.S. Navy and/or Marine Corps as officers, for immediate stationing in the war.
- December 21
  - Thailand and Japan sign a military alliance.
  - The Holocaust: Stanisławów Ghetto established.
- December 22 – WWII: Arcadia Conference opens in Washington, D.C., the first meeting on military strategy between the heads of government of the United Kingdom and the United States following the latter's entry into the war.

- December 23 – WWII: A second Japanese landing attempt on Wake Island is successful, and the American garrison surrenders after a full night and morning of fighting.
- December 24 – WWII:
  - British forces capture Benghazi.
  - Dutch submarine HNLMS K XVI is the first Allied ship to sink a Japanese warship, sinking the destroyer *Sagiri* near Sarawak; K XVI is herself torpedoed the following day by Japanese submarine I 66.
- December 25 – WWII:
  - The Battle of Hong Kong ends after 17 days with surrender of the British Crown colony to the Japanese.
  - Admiral Émile Muselier seizes the archipelago of Saint Pierre and Miquelon, the first part of France to be liberated by the Free French Forces.
- December 26 – WWII: Winston Churchill becomes the first British Prime Minister to address a joint session of the United States Congress.
- December 27 – WWII: British Commandos raid the Norwegian port of Vaagso, causing Hitler to reinforce the garrison and defenses, drawing vital troops away from other areas.

Date unknown

- *Classic Comics* series launched in the United States with a version of *The Three Musketeers*.

Births

January

Hayao Miyazaki

Joan Baez

Long John Baldry

Neil Diamond

Scott Glenn

Dick Cheney

- January 1
  - Dardo Cabo, Argentine journalist and activist (d. 1977)
  - Martin Evans, Welsh biologist awarded the Nobel Prize in Physiology or Medicine
- January 5 – Hayao Miyazaki, Japanese film director
- January 7
  - Iona Brown, British violinist and conductor (d. 2004)

- Manfred Schellscheidt, German American soccer coach
- John E. Walker, English chemist, Nobel Prize laureate
- January 8 – Graham Chapman, English comedian (d. 1989)
- January 9 – Joan Baez, American singer and activist
- January 11
  - Dave Edwards, American musician (d. 2000)
  - Jimmy Velvit, American singer/songwriter
- January 12 – Long John Baldry, British singer (d. 2005)
- January 14
  - Faye Dunaway, American actress
  - Milan Kučan, Slovenian politician and statesman
- January 15 – Captain Beefheart, American singer (d. 2010)
- January 18 – David Ruffin, American singer (The Temptations) (d. 1991)
- January 19 – Pat Patterson, Canadian professional wrestler
- January 20
  - Clift Tsuji, American politician
  - Allan Young, English footballer (d. 2009)
- January 21
  - Plácido Domingo, Spanish-born tenor
  - Richie Havens, American musician (d. 2013)
- January 24
  - Neil Diamond, American singer-songwriter
  - Aaron Neville, American singer
  - Dan Shechtman, Israeli chemist, Nobel Prize laureate
- January 25 – Theo Berger, German criminal
- January 26 – Scott Glenn, American actor
- January 27 – Beatrice Tinsley, English astronomer (d. 1981)
- January 30

- Dick Cheney, American politician (R-WY); 46th Vice President of the United States
  - Tineke Lagerberg, Dutch swimmer
- January 31
  - Lynne Abraham, American lawyer; former District Attorney of Philadelphia (1991–2010)
  - Dick Gephardt, American politician
  - Eugène Terre'Blanche, South African pro-apartheid politician, farmer (d. 2010)
  - Jessica Walter, American actress

February

Nick Nolte

- February 1
  - Jerry Spinelli, American children's author
  - Karl Dall, German comedian, singer and television presenter
- February 3
  - Dory Funk, Jr., American professional wrestler
  - Howard Phillips, American politician
- February 5

- o Stephen J. Cannell, American director and producer (d. 2010)
- o David Selby, American actor
- o Kaspar Villiger, Swiss politician
- February 8 – Nick Nolte, American actor
- February 10 – Michael Apted, English film director
- February 12 – Naomi Uemura, Japanese adventurer (d. 1984)
- February 13
  - o David Jeremiah, American televangelist
  - o Sigmar Polke, German painter
- February 19 – David Gross, American physicist, Nobel Prize laureate
- February 20 – Buffy Sainte-Marie, Canadian singer
- February 22 – Hipólito Mejía, President of the Dominican Republic
- February 27 – Lord Ashdown, British politician and life peer
- February 28 – Suzanne Mubarak, Egyptian first lady

March

Richard Dawkins

- March 1 – Joo Hyun, South Korean actor
- March 4
  - o John Aprea, American actor

- o Adrian Lyne, English film director
- March 9 – Ernesto Miranda, American criminal (d. 1976)
- March 12 – Erkki Salmenhaara, Finnish composer (d. 2002)
- March 14 – Wolfgang Petersen, German film director
- March 15 – Mike Love, American musician
- March 16
  - o Robert Guéï, military ruler of Côte d'Ivoire (d. 2002)
  - o Chuck Woolery, American game show host
- March 17 – Paul Kantner, American rock guitarist (d. 2016)
- March 18 – Wilson Pickett, American singer (d. 2006)
- March 20 – Kenji Kimihara, Japanese long-distance runner
- March 23 – Jim Trelease, American educator and author
- March 26 – Richard Dawkins, British scientist
- March 28
  - o Philip Fang, Hong Kong simultaneous interpretation specialist, United Nations official (d. 2013)
  - o Jim Turner, American football player
- March 29 – Joseph Hooton Taylor, Jr., American astrophysicist, Nobel Prize laureate
- March 30
  - o Wasim Sajjad, President of Pakistan
  - o Graeme Edge, English rock drummer and songwriter (The Moody Blues)

April

Michael D. Higgins

- April 2 – Dr. Demento (né Barret Eugene Hansen), American radio disc jockey, novelty music collector
- April 3
  - Eric Braeden, German-born American actor
  - Jorma Hynninen, Finnish baritone
  - Philippé Wynne, American musician (d. 1984)
- April 8 – Peggy Lennon, American singer (The Lennon Sisters)
- April 9 – Kay Adams, American country singer
- April 11 – Shirley Stelfox, English actress (d. 2015)
- April 12 – Bobby Moore, English football player; World Cup winning captain (d. 1993)
- April 13 – Michael Stuart Brown, American geneticist, recipient of the Nobel Prize in Physiology or Medicine
- April 14 – Pete Rose, American baseball player
- April 18 – Michael D. Higgins, 9th President of Ireland
- April 20 – Ryan O'Neal, American actor
- April 21 – David L. Boren, U.S. Senator from Oklahoma
- April 23

- Paavo Lipponen, Prime Minister of Finland
  - Ed Stewart, English disc jockey (d. 2016)
  - Ray Tomlinson, American computer programmer (d. 2016)
- April 24
  - Richard Holbrooke, American diplomat (d. 2010)
  - John Williams, Australian guitarist
- April 27 – Lee Roy Jordan, American football player
- April 28
  - Ann-Margret, Swedish-born American actress, singer and dancer
  - K. Barry Sharpless, American chemist, Nobel Prize laureate
  - Iryna Zhylenko, Ukrainian poet (d. 2013)

May

Bob Dylan

- May 3 – Nona Gaprindashvili, Georgian chess player
- May 5 – Alexander Ragulin, Russian hockey player (d. 2004)
- May 6 – Ivica Osim, Bosnian football player and manager
- May 11 – Eric Burdon, English singer
- May 13

- o Senta Berger, Austrian actress
  - o Ritchie Valens, American singer (d. 1959)
- May 19
  - o Bobby Burgess, American dancer and singer
  - o Nora Ephron, American film producer, director, and screenwriter (d. 2012)
- May 20 – Goh Chok Tong, Prime Minister of Singapore
- May 21 – Bobby Cox, American baseball manager
- May 22 – Menzies Campbell, British politician
- May 24 – Bob Dylan, American poet and musician
- May 26 – John Kaufman, English sculptor
- May 27 – Teppo Hauta-aho, Finnish double bassist and composer
- May 31 – Louis Ignarro, American pharmacologist, recipient of the Nobel Prize in Physiology or Medicine

June

Stacy Keach

Charlie Watts

Otto Sander

- June 1
  - Wayne Kemp, American country music singer (d. 2015)
  - Alexander Zakharov, Soviet (later Russian) deputy scientist and astronomer
- June 2
  - Stacy Keach, American actor
  - Charlie Watts, English musician (The Rolling Stones)
- June 5
  - Martha Argerich, Argentine pianist
  - Spalding Gray, American actor and screenwriter (d. 2004)
- June 7 – Tony Ray-Jones, British photographer (d. 1972)

- June 8
  - Robert Bradford, Northern Irish politician (d. 1981)
  - Fuzzy Haskins, American musician (P-Funk)
- June 9 – Jon Lord, organist of Deep Purple (d. 2012)
- June 10
  - Mickey Jones, American actor and musician
  - James A. Paul, American writer and non-profit executive
  - Jürgen Prochnow, German actor
- June 12 – Marv Albert, American sports announcer
- June 14 – Roy Harper, English guitarist
- June 15
  - Neal Adams, American comic book artist
  - Harry Nilsson, American musician (d. 1994)
- June 16
  - Rosalind Baker, Australian author
- June 19
  - Conchita Carpio-Morales, Filipino Supreme Court jurist
  - Václav Klaus, President of the Czech Republic
- June 21
  - Joe Flaherty, American-Canadian actor and comedian
  - Valeri Zolotukhin, Soviet/Russian actor
- June 22
  - Ed Bradley, American journalist (d. 2006)
  - Michael Lerner, American actor
  - Terttu Savola, Finnish politician
- June 24
  - Erkin Koray, Turkish musician
  - Bill Reardon, American politician and educator
  - Charles Whitman, American mass murderer (d. 1966)

- June 27 – Krzysztof Kieślowski, Polish film director (d. 1996)
- June 28
    - Joseph Goguen, American computer scientist (d. 2006)
    - David Johnston, 28th Governor General of Canada
- June 30 – Otto Sander, German actor (d. 2013)

July

Paul Anka

- July 1
    - Alfred G. Gilman, American scientist, recipient of the Nobel Prize in Physiology or Medicine (d. 2015)
    - Myron Scholes, American economist, Nobel Prize laureate
- July 6 – Harold Leighton Weller, American conductor
- July 7
    - Michael Howard, Baron Howard of Lympne, Welsh politician
    - Bill Oddie, English writer, composer, musician, comedian
- July 10 – Jackie Lane, English actress
- July 11 – Tommy Vance, English disc jockey (d. 2005)
- July 12
    - John Lahr, American drama critic
    - Benny Parsons, American race car driver (d. 2007)

- July 14
  - Maulana Karenga, American author and activist
  - Andreas Khol, Austrian politician
- July 16 – Hans Wiegel, Dutch politician
- July 18 – Frank Farian, German record producer and songwriter
- July 19
  - Vikki Carr, American singer
  - Neelie Kroes, Dutch politician
- July 22 – George Clinton, American musician
- July 23 – Sergio Mattarella, Italian lawyer, judge and politician, 12th President of Italy
- July 27 – Bill Baxley, Alabama politician
- July 28
  - Peter Cullen, Canadian voice actor
  - Riccardo Muti, Italian conductor
- July 29
  - Jennifer Dunn, American politician (d. 2007)
  - David Warner, English actor
- July 30 – Paul Anka, Canadian-American singer and songwriter
- July 31 – Amarsinh Chaudhary, Indian politician

August

Martha Stewart

- August 2 – Ede Staal, Dutch singer-songwriter
- August 3
  - Martha Stewart, American television personality and media entrepreneur
  - Hage Geingob, President of Namibia
- August 4 – Ted Strickland, American politician
- August 6 – Lyle Berman, American poker player
- August 8 – George Tiller, American physician (d. 2009)
- August 9 – Shirlee Busbee, American novelist.
- August 12 – Deborah Walley, American actress (d. 2001)
- August 14
  - David Crosby, American musician
  - Connie Smith, American singer
- August 16
  - Théoneste Bagosora, former Rwandan army officer and alleged planner of the Rwandan Genocide
  - David Dickinson, British antiques expert and television presenter

- August 17
  - Ibrahim Babangida, former President of Nigeria
  - Lothar Bisky, German politician (d. 2013)
  - Fritz Wepper, German actor
- August 20 – Slobodan Milošević, President of Serbia (d. 2006)

September

Bernie Sanders

Ahmet Necdet Sezer

- September 1 – George Saimes, American football player
- September 2
  - David Bale, South African-born businessman; father of actor Christian Bale and husband of feminist activist Gloria Steinem (d. 2003)

- Jyrki Otila, Finnish quiz show judge and Member of the European Parliament (d. 2003)
  - John Thompson, American basketball coach
- September 3 – Sergei Dovlatov, Russian short-story writer and novelist (d. 1990)
- September 4 – Sushilkumar Shinde, Indian politician
- September 8 – Bernie Sanders, American politician
- September 9
  - Otis Redding, American musician (d. 1967)
  - Dennis Ritchie, American computer scientist (d. 2011)
- September 10
  - Christopher Hogwood, English conductor and harpsichordist (d. 2014)
  - Gunpei Yokoi, Japanese computer game producer (d. 1997)
- September 13
  - Tadao Ando, Japanese architect
  - Ahmet Necdet Sezer, former President of Turkey
- September 14 – Alberto Naranjo, Venezuelan musician
- September 15 – Mirosław Hermaszewski, first Polish cosmonaut in space
- September 17 – Bob Matsui, U.S. Congressman from California (d. 2005)
- September 19 – Cass Elliot, American singer (d. 1974)
- September 20 – Dale Chihuly, American glass sculptor
- September 24
  - Guy Hovis, American singer
  - Linda McCartney, American activist, musician and photographer (d. 1998)
- September 26 – Martine Beswick, British actress and model

- September 27
  - Gay Kayler Ashcroft, Australian country music singer
  - Sam Zell, American publisher and investor
- September 28 – Edmund Stoiber, German politician
- September 29 – Fred West, English serial killer (d. 1995)
- September 30 – Angela Pleasence, English actress

October

Paul Simon

- October 2 – Zareh Baronian, Archimandrite theologian
- October 3 – Chubby Checker, American singer
- October 4
  - Roy Blount, Jr., American writer and comedian
  - Elizabeth Eckford, American activist
  - Anne Rice, American writer
- October 5 – Eduardo Duhalde, President of Argentina
- October 8 – Jesse Jackson, American clergyman and civil rights activist
- October 9 – Trent Lott, former United States Senator (R-MS)
- October 10 – Peter Coyote, American actor
- October 13 – Paul Simon, American singer and composer
- October 16 – Tim McCarver, American baseball commentator

- October 20 – Anneke Wills, British actress
- October 23 – Mel Winkler, American actor
- October 25
  - Helen Reddy, Australian singer and actress
  - Anne Tyler, American novelist
- October 27 – Gerd Brantenberg, Norwegian feminist author and gay rights activist
- October 28
  - John Hallam, Irish actor
  - Jochen Hasenmayer, German cave diver
  - Hank Marvin, British guitarist, singer and songwriter (The Shadows)
- October 30 – Theodor W. Hänsch, German physicist, Nobel Prize in Physics
- October 31 – Sally Kirkland, American actress

November

Art Garfunkel

- November 1
  - Marina Baura, Spanish-Venezuelan film and television actress
  - Nigel Dempster, British journalist, author, broadcaster and diarist (d. 2007)

- o Robert Foxworth, American actor
- November 2 – Bruce Welch, British guitarist, singer and songwriter
- November 5 – Art Garfunkel, American singer
- November 6 – Doug Sahm, American musician (d. 1999)
- November 7 – Angelo Scola, Italian cardinal
- November 9 – Tom Fogerty, American guitarist (Creedence Clearwater Revival) (d. 1990)
- November 17 – Tova Traesnaes, Norwegian-American cosmetician and businesswoman; widow of actor Ernest Borgnine
- November 18 – David Hemmings, English actor (d. 2003)
- November 19 – Dan Haggerty, American actor (d. 2016)
- November 21 – Juliet Mills, English actress
- November 23 – Derek Mahon, Irish poet
- November 24 – Pete Best, English drummer
- November 25
  - o Ralph Haben, American politician, former Speaker of the Florida House of Representatives
  - o Riaz Ahmed Gohar Shahi, Sufi, author, poet
- November 26 – G. Alan Marlatt, Canadian-born American psychologist
- November 27 – Eddie Rabbitt, American country musician (d. 1998)
- November 28 – Laura Antonelli, Italian actress (d. 2015)
- November 29 – Bill Freehan, American baseball player

December

Lee Myung-bak

Sir Alex Ferguson

- December 4 – David Johnston, Australian newsreader
- December 6
  - Vittorio Mezzogiorno, Italian actor (d. 1994)
  - Richard Speck, American mass murderer (d. 1991)
- December 9 – Beau Bridges, American actor
- December 10 – Kyu Sakamoto, Japanese singer and actor (d. 1985)
- December 11 – J. Frank Wilson, American singer (J. Frank Wilson and the Cavaliers) (d. 1991)
- December 13 – John Davidson, American singer and actor

- December 18 – Prince William of Gloucester, member of the English royal family
- December 19
  - Lee Myung-bak, 17th President of South Korea
  - Maurice White, American singer, songwriter, musician and record producer, founder of Earth, Wind & Fire (d. 2016)
- December 21 – Lo Hoi-pang, Hong Kong-born Chinese actor
- December 23
  - Ron Bushy, American rock musician
  - Tim Hardin, American musician (d. 1980)
- December 24 – John Levene, English actor
- December 27 – Miles Aiken, American basketball player and coach
- December 30 – Mel Renfro, American football player
- December 31 – Sir Alex Ferguson, Scottish football manager (Manchester United)

Deaths

January

- January 1 – József Konkolics, Hungarian Slovene writer (d. 1861)
- January 4 – Henri Bergson, French philosopher, recipient of the Nobel Prize in Literature (b. 1859)
- January 5 – Amy Johnson, English aviator (b. 1903)

- January 8 – Lord Robert Baden-Powell, English soldier and founder of the Boy Scouts (b. 1857)
- January 10
  - Frank Bridge, English composer (b. 1879)
  - Sir John Lavery, Anglo-Irish artist (b. 1856)
  - Joe Penner, Hungarian-born American comedic actor (b. 1904)
- January 13 – James Joyce, Irish writer and poet (b. 1882)
- January 29 – Ioannis Metaxas, dictator of Greece (b. 1871)

February

Frederick Banting

- February 2 – Harris Laning, American admiral (b. 1873)
- February 6 – Banjo Paterson, Australian poet and journalist (b. 1864)
- February 7 – Giuseppe Tellera, Italian general (died of wounds) (b. 1882)
- February 9 – Aaron S. Watkins, American temperance movement leader (b. 1863)
- February 11 – Rudolf Hilferding, German economist and Minister of Finance (b. 1877)

- February 21 – Frederick Banting, Canadian physician, recipient of the Nobel Prize in Physiology or Medicine (b. 1891)
- February 24 – Lothar von Arnauld de la Perière, German submarine commander (b. 1886)
- February 27 – William D. Byron, U.S. Congressman (b. 1895)
- February 28 – King Alfonso XIII of Spain (b. 1886)

March

- March 6 – Gutzon Borglum, American sculptor (*Mount Rushmore*) (b. 1867)
- March 7 – Günther Prien, German submarine commander (killed in action) (b. 1908)
- March 8 – Sherwood Anderson, American author (b. 1876)
- March 15 – Alexej von Jawlensky, Russian painter (b. 1864)
- March 17 – Joachim Schepke, German submarine commander (killed in action) (b. 1912)
- March 28
  - Kavasji Jamshedji Petigara, Indian police commissioner (b. 1887)
  - Virginia Woolf, English writer (b. 1882)
- March 30 – Vasil Kutinchev, Bulgarian general (b. 1859)

April

- April 5 – Sir Nigel Gresley, English steam locomotive engineer (*Flying Scotsman* and *Mallard*) (b. 1876)
- April 13 – Annie Jump Cannon, American astronomer (b. 1863)

- April 16 – Josiah Stamp, British baron, banker, civil servant, industrialist, economist and statistician (b.1880)
- April 24 – Karin Boye, Swedish poetess (suicide) (b. 1900)
- April 30 – Edwin S. Porter, American film director (b. 1870)

May

- May 6 – Shūzō Kuki, Japanese philosopher (b. 1888)
- May 7 – James George Frazer, Scottish social anthropologist (b. 1854)
- May 11 – Peggy Shannon, American actress (b. 1910)
- May 12 – Ruth Stonehouse, American actress (b. 1892)
- May 16 – Minnie Vautrin, American missionary and heroine of the Nanjing Massacre (b. 1887)
- May 24 – Lancelot Holland, British admiral (b. 1887)
- May 27 – Günther Lütjens, German admiral (b. 1889)
- May 30 – Prajadhipok, Rama VII, king of Thailand (b. 1893)

June

Hans Berger

Wilhelm II

- June 1
  - Hans Berger, German neurologist (b. 1873)
  - Jenny Dolly, American singer (b. 1892)
  - Hugh Walpole, British writer (b. 1884)
- June 2 – Lou Gehrig, American baseball player and MLB Hall of Famer (b. 1903)
- June 4 – Wilhelm II, last Emperor of Germany (b. 1859)
- June 6 – Louis Chevrolet, Swiss-born automobile builder and race car driver (b. 1878)
- June 15 – Evelyn Underhill, British writer (b. 1875)
- June 21 – Elliott Dexter, American actor (b. 1870)
- June 29 – Ignacy Jan Paderewski, Polish pianist, composer, and third Prime Minister of Poland (b. 1860)

July

- July 3 – Friedrich Akel, Estonian diplomat and politician (b. 1871)
- July 4 – Antoni Łomnicki, Polish mathematician (b. 1881)

- July 10 – Jelly Roll Morton, African-American jazz musician and composer (b. 1890)
- July 11 – Arthur Evans, English archaeologist (b. 1851)
- July 15 – Walter Ruttmann, German director (b. 1887)
- July 20 – Lew Fields, American vaudeville performer (b. 1867)
- July 23 – José Quiñones Gonzales, Peruvian aviator (b. 1914)
- July 24 – Rudolf Ramek, 6th Chancellor of Austria (b. 1881)
- July 25 – Allan Forrest, American actor (b. 1885)
- July 26 – Henri Lebesgue, French mathematician (b. 1875)
- July 29 – James Stephenson, British actor (b. 1889)
- July 30 – Mickey Welch, American baseball player and MLB Hall of Famer (b. 1859)

August

- August 7 – Rabindranath Tagore, Indian author, Nobel Prize laureate (b. 1861)
- August 13 – James Stuart Blackton, American film producer (b. 1875)
- August 14
  - Paul Sabatier, French chemist, Nobel Prize laureate (b. 1854)
  - Maximilian Kolbe, German Franciscan (voluntary execution) (b. 1894)
- August 20 – John Baird, 1st Viscount Stonehaven, British politician, former Governor-General of Australia (b. 1874)
- August 30 – Peder Oluf Pedersen, Danish engineer and physicist (b. 1874)

- August 31 – Marina Tsvetaeva, Russian poet (suicide) (b. 1892)

September

Hans Spemann

- September 1 – Karl Parts, Estonian military commander (b. 1886)
- September 9 – Hans Spemann, German embryologist, recipient of the Nobel Prize in Physiology or Medicine (b. 1869)
- September 18 – Fred Karno, British music hall comedian (b. 1866)
- September 20 – Mikhail Kirponos, Soviet general (killed in action) (b. 1892)

October

- October 5 – Louis Brandeis, U.S. Supreme Court Justice (b. 1856)
- October 8
  - Gus Kahn, German songwriter (b. 1886)
  - Valentine O'Hara, Irish author (b. 1875)

- October 9 – Helen Morgan, American singer and actress (b. 1900)
- October 25 – Robert Delaunay, French painter (b. 1885)
- October 26
    - Arkady Gaidar, Russian writer (b. 1904)
    - Victor Schertzinger, American composer and director (b. 1888)
- October 29 – Harvey Hendrick, American baseball player (b. 1897)

November

Walther Nernst

- November 16 – Miina Härma, Estonian composer (b. 1864)
- November 17 – Ernst Udet, German World War I fighter ace and Nazi *Luftwaffe* official (suicide) (b. 1896)
- November 18
    - Émile Nelligan, Canadian poet (b. 1879)
    - Walther Nernst, German chemist, Nobel Prize laureate (b. 1864)
    - Chris Watson, 3rd Prime Minister of Australia (b. 1867)
- November 22
    - Werner Mölders, German fighter pilot (b. 1913)
    - Kurt Koffka, German psychologist (b. 1886)

- November 23 – Henrietta Vinton Davis, American elocutionist, dramatist, impersonator, public speaker (b. 1860)
- November 25 – Pedro Aguirre Cerda, President of Chile (b. 1879)
- November 26 – Niels Hansen Jacobsen, Danish sculptor and ceramist (b. 1861)
- November 27 – Charles James Briggs, British general (b. 1865)
- November 30 – Esmond Romilly, British socialist (b. 1918)

December

- December 2 – Edward Rydz-Śmigły, Polish marshal (b. 1886)
- December 3 – Christian Sinding, Norwegian composer (b. 1856)
- December 7 – Isaac Campbell Kidd, American admiral (b. 1884)
- December 9 – Eduard von Böhm-Ermolli, Austrian general and German field marshal (b. 1856)
- December 10 – Tom Phillips, British admiral (b. 1888)
- December 11 – Émile Picard, French mathematician (b. 1856)
- December 12 – César Basa, Filipino pilot (b. 1915)
- December 25 – Blanche Bates, stage actress (b. 1873)
- December 29 – Tullio Levi-Civita, Italian mathematician (b. 1873)
- December 30 – El Lissitzky, Russian artist and architect (b. 1890)

Nobel Prizes

- Physics – not awarded
- Chemistry – not awarded
- Medicine – not awarded
- Literature – not awarded
- Peace – not awarded

In the News.

The war in Europe continues to escalate with countries joining on one side or the other.

In the North Atlantic, the German battleship Bismarck sinks the HMS Hood on May24th.

Nazi Germany launches Operation Barbarossa, the invasion of the Soviet Union.

The Mount. Rushmore sculpture featuring US Presidents is completed by Gutzon Borglum.

Rudolf Hess, parachuted into Scotland on a peace mission and is captured by British forces.

U.S. President Franklin D. Roosevelt is inaugurated for his 3rd term as US President.

The Enigma Code Is Broken.

Japanese Navy launches a surprise attack consisting by the Imperial Japanese Navy on December 7th of the United States fleet at Pearl Harbor, thus drawing the United States into World War II.

United Stated officially declares war on Japan.

Popular films - Citizen Kane, Dumbo, The Maltese Falcon.

Churchill launches the "V for Victory" campaign across Europe.

A bill creates the fourth Thursday in November as Thanksgiving Day.

Average Cost of new house $4,075.00

Average wages per year $1,750.00

Cost of a gallon of Gas 12 cents Average

Cost for house rent $32.00 per month

1941 Calendar

January 1941
Sun	Mon	Tue	Wed	Thu	Fri	Sat
			1	2	3	4
5	6	7	8	9	10	11
12	13	14	15	16	17	18
19	20	21	22	23	24	25
26	27	28	29	30	31	

February 1941
Sun	Mon	Tue	Wed	Thu	Fri	Sat
						1
2	3	4	5	6	7	8
9	10	11	12	13	14	15
16	17	18	19	20	21	22
23	24	25	26	27	28	

March 1941
Sun	Mon	Tue	Wed	Thu	Fri	Sat
						1
2	3	4	5	6	7	8
9	10	11	12	13	14	15
16	17	18	19	20	21	22
23	24	25	26	27	28	29
30	31					

April 1941
Sun	Mon	Tue	Wed	Thu	Fri	Sat
		1	2	3	4	5
6	7	8	9	10	11	12
13	14	15	16	17	18	19
20	21	22	23	24	25	26
27	28	29	30			

May 1941
Sun	Mon	Tue	Wed	Thu	Fri	Sat
				1	2	3
4	5	6	7	8	9	10
11	12	13	14	15	16	17
18	19	20	21	22	23	24
25	26	27	28	29	30	31

June 1941
Sun	Mon	Tue	Wed	Thu	Fri	Sat
1	2	3	4	5	6	7
8	9	10	11	12	13	14
15	16	17	18	19	20	21
22	23	24	25	26	27	28
29	30					

July 1941
Sun	Mon	Tue	Wed	Thu	Fri	Sat
		1	2	3	4	5
6	7	8	9	10	11	12
13	14	15	16	17	18	19
20	21	22	23	24	25	26
27	28	29	30	31		

August 1941
Sun	Mon	Tue	Wed	Thu	Fri	Sat
					1	2
3	4	5	6	7	8	9
10	11	12	13	14	15	16
17	18	19	20	21	22	23
24	25	26	27	28	29	30
31						

September 1941
Sun	Mon	Tue	Wed	Thu	Fri	Sat
	1	2	3	4	5	6
7	8	9	10	11	12	13
14	15	16	17	18	19	20
21	22	23	24	25	26	27
28	29	30				

October 1941
Sun	Mon	Tue	Wed	Thu	Fri	Sat
			1	2	3	4
5	6	7	8	9	10	11
12	13	14	15	16	17	18
19	20	21	22	23	24	25
26	27	28	29	30	31	

November 1941
Sun	Mon	Tue	Wed	Thu	Fri	Sat
						1
2	3	4	5	6	7	8
9	10	11	12	13	14	15
16	17	18	19	20	21	22
23	24	25	26	27	28	29
30						

December 1941
Sun	Mon	Tue	Wed	Thu	Fri	Sat
	1	2	3	4	5	6
7	8	9	10	11	12	13
14	15	16	17	18	19	20
21	22	23	24	25	26	27
28	29	30	31			

www.ingramcontent.com/pod-product-compliance
Lightning Source LLC
Chambersburg PA
CBHW071117280526
45787CB00003B/1078